Food Fractions

Learning How Fractional Parts Equal a Whole

Sharon Moore

Math
for the
REAL World™

Rosen Classroom Books & Materials
New York

Published in 2004 by The Rosen Publishing Group, Inc.
29 East 21st Street, New York, NY 10010

Book Design: Ron A. Churley

Photo Credits: Cover © StockFood; all interior photos by Maura B. McConnell.

ISBN: 0-8239-8852-X
6-pack ISBN: 0-8239-7329-8

Manufactured in the United States of America

Contents

Food Fractions

We use fractions every day when we are shopping, cooking, and eating. Fractions are parts of a whole. When you are shopping, you often buy parts of whole foods. You may want to buy $\frac{1}{2}$ pound of cheese instead of 1 whole pound. When you are cooking, you may use $\frac{1}{3}$ cup of sugar instead of 1 whole cup. When you are eating with 3 friends, you may want to **divide** a snack into 4 parts so that each person gets $\frac{1}{4}$.

When we use $\frac{1}{3}$ of a cup of sugar to make our favorite food, we are using a fraction, or a part, of 1 whole cup. When we divide a pizza into 4 equal parts to share with our friends, each person is each eating $\frac{1}{4}$ of the whole pizza.

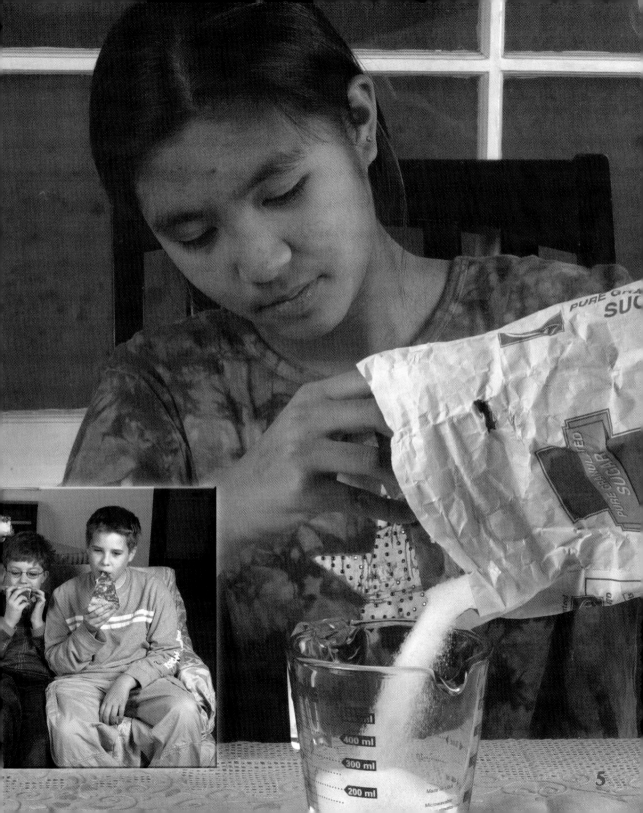

Equal Fractions

A fraction has 2 numbers. The bottom number shows the total number of **equal** parts. The top number tells how many parts are being used. These 2 numbers are **separated** by a line. When the top number and the bottom number of a fraction are the same, the fraction is equal to 1 whole.

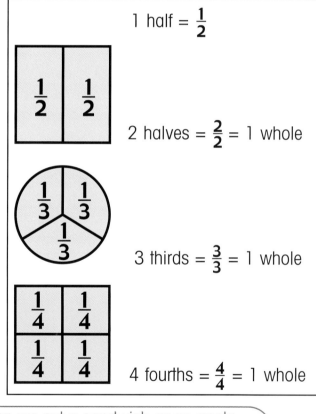

1 half = $\frac{1}{2}$

| $\frac{1}{2}$ | $\frac{1}{2}$ |

2 halves = $\frac{2}{2}$ = 1 whole

$\frac{1}{3}$ $\frac{1}{3}$ $\frac{1}{3}$

3 thirds = $\frac{3}{3}$ = 1 whole

| $\frac{1}{4}$ | $\frac{1}{4}$ |
| $\frac{1}{4}$ | $\frac{1}{4}$ |

4 fourths = $\frac{4}{4}$ = 1 whole

We use fractions when we cut a sandwich or an apple into 2 equal pieces. Each part is $\frac{1}{2}$ of the whole sandwich or apple. One whole is made up of 2 halves. The fractions 3 thirds ($\frac{3}{3}$) and 4 fourths ($\frac{4}{4}$) also equal 1 whole.

We can buy $\frac{1}{2}$ dozen eggs, $\frac{1}{2}$ pound of butter, or $\frac{1}{4}$ pound of meat at the store. What other kinds of foods can we buy in fractional parts?

Fractions at the Store

Jean goes to the store to buy food. She buys 1 gallon of milk. How many $\frac{1}{2}$ gallons are in 1 gallon of milk? There are 2 half gallons in 1 gallon of milk.

Jean only wants to buy $\frac{1}{4}$ pound of cheese instead of 1 whole pound. How many fourths are in 1 pound of cheese? There are 4 fourths ($\frac{4}{4}$) in 1 whole pound of cheese.

$$\frac{1}{2} + \frac{1}{2} = \frac{2}{2}$$

$\frac{1}{2}$ + $\frac{1}{2}$ = $\frac{2}{2}$ or 1 whole gallon

Fractions in Cooking

We use fractions when we are cooking. Many times we don't need 1 whole cup of an **ingredient**, just a fraction or part of a cup. Ann used $\frac{1}{3}$ cup of sugar to make cookies. How many thirds are equal to 1 cup? Three thirds ($\frac{3}{3}$) are equal to 1 cup of sugar. Bob used $\frac{1}{4}$ cup of oil to make brownies. How many fourths are equal to 1 cup? Four fourths ($\frac{4}{4}$) are equal to 1 cup.

We have learned that fractions like $\frac{3}{3}$ and $\frac{4}{4}$ are equal to 1. Did you know that fractions like $\frac{25}{25}$ or $\frac{100}{100}$ are also equal to 1?

$$\frac{1}{3} = \frac{1}{3} = \frac{1}{3} = 1 \text{ cup}$$

$$\frac{1}{3} + \frac{1}{3} + \frac{1}{3} = \frac{3}{3} \text{ or 1 cup}$$

$$\frac{1}{4} = \frac{1}{4} = \frac{1}{4} = \frac{1}{4} = 1 \text{ cup}$$

$$\frac{1}{4} + \frac{1}{4} + \frac{1}{4} + \frac{1}{4} = \frac{4}{4} \text{ or 1 cup}$$

Fractions in Foods We Eat

Bob has a candy bar to share with 3 of his friends. If he gives himself and each of his friends the same size piece, what fraction of the candy bar will each person get? The whole candy bar has 4 equal pieces, or 4 fourths ($\frac{4}{4}$). Each person will get $\frac{1}{4}$ of the whole candy bar.

Jan baked a pie. She cuts it into equal pieces for herself and 4 other people. What fraction of the pie will each person get?

$\frac{1}{4}$ $\frac{1}{4}$ $\frac{1}{4}$ $\frac{1}{4}$

$\frac{1}{4} + \frac{1}{4} + \frac{1}{4} + \frac{1}{4} = \frac{4}{4}$ or 1 whole candy bar

The whole pie is divided into 5 equal pieces, or 5 fifths ($\frac{5}{5}$). Each person will get $\frac{1}{5}$ of the whole pie.

$$\frac{1}{5} + \frac{1}{5} + \frac{1}{5} + \frac{1}{5} + \frac{1}{5} = \frac{5}{5} \text{ or 1 whole pie}$$

Adding Fractions

Sometimes we add fractions together to figure out how much more we will need to equal 1 whole. If you bought $\frac{2}{3}$ pound of brown sugar at the store, how many more thirds would you need to make 1 whole pound? The answer is $\frac{1}{3}$, because $\frac{2}{3} + \frac{1}{3} = \frac{3}{3}$ or 1. If you had $\frac{3}{4}$ cup of flour and needed 1 whole cup, how many fourths would you add? The answer is $\frac{1}{4}$, because $\frac{3}{4} + \frac{1}{4} = \frac{4}{4}$ or 1. What fractions do you find when you are shopping, cooking, and eating?

Glossary

divide (duh-VYD) To break something into equal parts.

equal (EE-kwuhl) The same in size, number, or amount.

ingredient (in-GREE-dee-uhnt) Any one of the foods that are part of a recipe.

separate (SEH-puh-rayt) To keep two things apart.

Index